Facts About the Swan

By Lisa Strattin

© 2019 Lisa Strattin

Facts for Kids Picture Books by Lisa Strattin

Little Blue Penguin, Vol 92

Chipmunk, Vol 5

Frilled Lizard, Vol 39

Blue and Gold Macaw, Vol 13

Poison Dart Frogs, Vol 50

Blue Tarantula, Vol 115

African Elephants, Vol 8

Amur Leopard, Vol 89

Sabre Tooth Tiger, Vol 167

Baboon, Vol 174

Sign Up for New Release Emails Here

http://LisaStrattin.com/subscribe-here

Monthly Surprise Box

http://KidCraftsByLisa.com

All rights reserved. No part of this book may be reproduced by any means whatsoever without the written permission from the author, except brief portions quoted for purpose of review.

All information in this book has been carefully researched and checked for factual accuracy. However, the author and publisher makes no warranty, express or implied, that the information contained herein is appropriate for every individual, situation or purpose and assume no responsibility for errors or omissions. The reader assumes the risk and full responsibility for all actions, and the author will not be held responsible for any loss or damage, whether consequential, incidental, special or otherwise, that may result from the information presented in this book.

All images are free for use or purchased from stock photo sites for commercial use.

Some coloring pages might be of the general species due to lack of available images.

I have relied on my own observations as well as many different sources for this book and I have done my best to check facts and give credit where it is due. In the event that any material is used without proper permission, please contact me so that the oversight can be corrected.

Contents

INTRODUCTION 7

CHARACTERISTICS 9

APPEARANCE 11

LIFE STAGES 13

LIFE SPAN 15

SIZE 17

HABITAT 19

DIET 21

FRIENDS AND ENEMIES 23

SUITABILITY AS PETS 25

PLUSH SWAN TOY 38

MONTHLY SURPRISE BOX 39

INTRODUCTION

The swan is a large water bird closely related to geese and ducks. It is known for a fierce temperament and incredibly strong wings which are able to cause injury to any animal that threatens.

The swan is found around the world, on both sides of the Equator across the Northern and Southern Hemispheres.

CHARACTERISTICS

The Australian black swan has been noted to only swim with one leg, the other being tucked above its tail. This helps to change direction more smoothly when the swan is swimming on the surface of the water, if the swan spots food or a predator.

Swans have adapted in order to survive life on the water. Their streamline body shape, long neck and webbed feet help them in their environment. The wings of the swan are also very strong, the swan is one of the few heavy birds that is able to fly, even if it is only a short distance at a time.

APPEARANCE

There are around 7 different species of swan found around the world. The size, color and behavior of a particular swan individual is largely dependent on its species and the area in which it lives.

The northern swan is usually white with an orange beak and the southern swan tends to be a mixture of white and black with red, orange or black beaks.

LIFE STAGES

Although swans do not mate for life, the couples do establish strong bonds between one another and can often stay together for a few years. They build their nests on land out of twigs and leaves, and the female lays between 3 and 9 eggs.

The baby swans, known as cygnets, hatch out of their eggs after incubation of just over a month. They are often on the water with their mother within a couple of days and stay close to her for both protection and warmth while young.

The mother swan guards her babies from predators or any animal that she believes is a threat.

LIFE SPAN

Swans live for around 8 to 12 years, in the wild.

SIZE

An adult swan is 3 to 5 feet tall and weighs between 20 to 35 pounds.

HABITAT

Swans are termed waterfowl, and rely on bodies of water to be their environment. They live in a variety of areas with water, including lakes, ponds, slow moving rivers and streams, wetlands, marshes, and more. When nesting, these birds usually choose sites on land in near water.

DIET

Swans are omnivorous birds but have a mostly vegetarian diet. They eat underwater vegetation like seaweed and aquatic plants when they are on the water, and a mixture of plants, seeds and berries when on land. They also eat insects in the water and on land and occasionally small fish as well.

FRIENDS AND ENEMIES

Because they are large and strong, swans have only a few natural predators in the wild. Several predators of the swan include wolves, raccoons and foxes; these animals prey both on the swan itself and also its eggs.

Humans can be friends to swans, we like to watch them on the water. They are considered very graceful and calming to watch.

SUITABILITY AS PETS

Since the swan can be a bit testy, it's not a particularly good choice for a pet. Plus, since they can fly away, it would be hard to keep one in your backyard pond. If you have a large pond at your house, though, you might end up seeing a swan or two living there. As long as the swan doesn't feel threatened, it could stay there for a long time. However, assuming you don't have a large pond, you can probably go see some swans at the zoo in your city and watch them there.

COLOR ME

COLOR ME

COLOR ME

COLOR ME

COLOR ME

COLOR ME

COLOR ME

COLOR ME

COLOR ME

COLOR ME

Please leave me a review here:

http://lisastrattin.com/Review-Vol-213

For more Kindle Downloads Visit Lisa Strattin Author Page on Amazon Author Central

http://amazon.com/author/lisastrattin

To see upcoming titles, visit my website at LisaStrattin.com– all books available on kindle!

http://lisastrattin.com

PLUSH SWAN TOY

You can get one by copying and pasting this link into your browser:

http://lisastrattin.com/PlushSwan

MONTHLY SURPRISE BOX

Get yours by copying and pasting this link into your browser

http://KidCraftsByLisa.com

Made in the USA
Coppell, TX
20 January 2020

14724495R00024